RUBANK Treasures
for TENOR SAXOPHONE

ONLINE MEDIA INCLUDED
Audio Recordings
Printable Piano Accompaniments

PLAYBACK➕
Speed • Pitch • Balance • Loop

CONTENTS

To access recordings and PDF piano accompaniments, go to:
www.halleonard.com/mylibrary

Enter Code
3484-7232-0934-9822

ISBN 978-1-4803-5244-5

RUBANK®

HAL•LEONARD®
7777 W. BLUEMOUND RD. P.O. BOX 13819 MILWAUKEE, WI 53213

T0050641

Copyright ©2018 by HAL LEONARD CORPORATION
International Copyright Secured   All Rights Reserved

Visit Hal Leonard Online at
www.halleonard.com

Sarabanda and Gavotta

Bb Tenor Saxophone

Arcangelo Corelli
Edited by H. Voxman

Night Piece

B♭ Tenor Saxophone

Leroy Ostransky

00121409

March of a Marionette

4

Bb Tenor Saxophone

Charles Gounod
Arranged by Harold L. Walters

00121409

Largo and Allegro

Bb Tenor Saxophone

Pietro Boni
Transcribed by H. Voxman

Intermezzo

Bb Tenor Saxophone

Paul Koepke

Sinfonia (Arioso)
from Cantata No. 156

Bb Tenor Saxophone

J.S. Bach
Transcribed by H. Voxman

This Cantata was composed by Bach ca. 1730. The original scoring of the Sinfonia is for solo oboe, strings, and continuo. The eighth-note accompaniment figures (treble) should probably be played quasi pizzicato. Bach also used this melody in a more elaborate version in his F minor Concerto for Clavier.

Waltz Moods

B♭ Tenor Saxophone

Clair W. Johnson

00121409

11

00121409

Berceuse

Bb Tenor Saxophone

J.Ed. Barat
Adapted by H. Voxman

Alleluja
from *Exsultate, Jubilate, K. 165*

Bb Tenor Saxophone

W.A. Mozart
Arranged by Clair W. Johnson

* Trills may be omitted.

Crépuscule
(Twilight)

Bb Tenor Saxophone

Gabriel Parès
Transcribed by R.A. Judy

00121409

* For ease of following, metronome clicks are provided in mm. 24-34 of the accompaniment-only recording.

Orientale

Bb Tenor Saxophone

J.Ed. Barat
Edited by H. Voxman

00121409

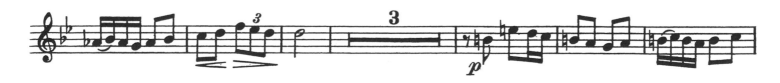

Prelude and Allegro

Bb Tenor Saxophone

Leroy Ostransky

* Designates a recording "click"
(accompaniment recording only)

Estilian Caprice

B♭ Tenor Saxophone

Gene Paul